Presented to:

....

From

....

Date

....

Books by Kevin Johnson

Early Teen Devotionals

Can I Be a Christian Without Being Weird?
Could Someone Wake Me Up Before I Drool on the Desk?
Does Anybody Know What Planet My Parents Are From?
So Who Says I Have to Act My Age?
Was That a Balloon or Did Your Head Just Pop?
Who Should I Listen To?
Why Can't My Life Be a Summer Vacation?
Why Is God Looking for Friends?

Early Teen Discipleship

Get God: Make Friends With the King of the Universe
Wise Up: Stand Clear of the Unsmartness of Sin
Cross Train: Blast Through the Bible From Front to Back
Pray Hard: Talk to God With Total Confidence

Books for Youth

Catch the Wave!
Find Your Fit[1]
God's Will, God's Best[2]
Jesus Among Other Gods: Youth Edition[3]
Look Who's Toast Now!
What Do Ya Know?
What's With the Dudes at the Door?[4]
What's With the Mutant in the Microscope?[4]
Where Ya Gonna Go?

*To find out more about Kevin Johnson's books
or speaking availability visit his Web site:
www.thewave.org*

[1]with Jane Kise [2]with Josh McDowell [3]with Ravi Zacharias [4]with James White

WHERE Ya Gonna GO?

NOW THAT YOU'RE A GRADUATE

KEVIN JOHNSON

BETHANYHOUSE

MINNEAPOLIS, MINNESOTA

Published by Bethany House Publishers
A Ministry of Bethany Fellowship International
11400 Hampshire Avenue South
Bloomington, Minnesota 55438
www.bethanyhouse.com

Printed in the United States of America

Library of Congress Cataloging-in-Publication Data

Johnson, Kevin (Kevin Walter)
    Where ya gonna go? : now you're a graduate / by Kevin Johnson.
       p.   cm.
    ISBN 0-7642-2340-2
    1. Christian life. 2. Young adults—Religious life. 3. Young adults—Conduct of life. I. Title.
    BV4529.2 .J66   2001
    248.8'3—dc21
                                          00-012969

To grads everywhere
who gladly go
wherever God
leads them.

Congrats!

KEVIN JOHNSON is the bestselling author of more than twenty books for youth, including *Can I Be a Christian Without Being Weird?* and *Catch the Wave!* A full-time author and speaker, he served as senior editor for adult nonfiction at Bethany House Publishers and pastored a group of more than four hundred sixth through ninth graders at Elmbrook Church in metro Milwaukee. While his training includes an M.Div. from Fuller Theological Seminary and a B.A. in English and Print Journalism from the University of Wisconsin–River Falls, his current interests include cycling, guitar, and shortwave radio. Kevin and his wife, Lyn, live in Minnesota with their three children — Nate, Karin, and Elise.

Contents

WHO ARE YOU?

PART ONE

YOUR IDENTITY, PURPOSE, AND VISION

Know it or not, you have a dream for your life. Even if you can't stand up and explain it to all the people who offer you congrats at your graduation, you're living your dream. It's where you're going with your life. Good or bad. Crazed or lazy. Got-it or just-want-it. Chase-it-hard or just-let-it-happen.

Call it your "lifedream." It's what you're spending your life trying to achieve.

You don't pick a lifedream thinking it will mess you up. But the wrong dreams are like sand castles. They dissolve into nothingness when a wave washes ashore.

You want a lifedream that survives and satisfies.

But you might not think to make following God the center of your dream.

God is bigger than anything else imaginable. He is Ultimate Power, Ultimate Intelligence, Ultimate Justice, and Ultimate Love. God burst into history in the person of Jesus Christ to wrap you and your world in total care, total wisdom, total fairness, and total belonging. He wants you to know Him. And He wants to make you part of His plan for the world.

A dream is only real if someone is big enough to make the dream come true. Jesus is big enough. And He says that total satisfaction flows from a relationship with Him (John 4:14).

As you choose where you're going you *can* choose what's most important. You *can* choose the lifedream that works. You *can* choose the one that's true and right.

Choose God.

Take delight in the Lord, and he will give you your heart's desires. Commit everything you do to the Lord. Trust him, and he will help you.

—PSALM 37:4–5 NLT

Maybe you've watched peers get accepted to prestigious schools and score fantastic scholarships. Others might have walked off the graduation platform straight into decent jobs. They ooze confidence and optimism—and that might make you doubt your own ability to cut the pressure of life after high school.

God thinks better thoughts about you.

God created you so you would reflect His greatness the way the moon—which makes no light of its own—reflects the light of the sun. He gave you the privilege of knowing, obeying, and worshiping Him, the God of the Universe. He made human beings responsible for ruling the world.

You probably think stuff you make is stupid—a clay pot in art class, a napkin holder from shop, a report for English. But God was very pleased when He made you (Genesis 1:31).

Even on days when you look at your life and think

you're nothing more than a mud splat, you're way more. You're God's masterpiece.

But why are people important to you? Why do you take care of human beings? You made them a little lower than the angels and crowned them with glory and honor.

— PSALM 8:3–4 NCV

Life is a string of events in which others do for you what you can't do—and teach you what you don't know—until you grow capable yourself.

As much as you're supposed to be all grown-up after graduation, sooner or later you have to admit it: Sometimes, in some situations, you're helpless and dumb.

Don't feel bad. So is everyone else. And being slick at covering it up isn't always a good thing.

Like every other human being on this planet, you need what God wants to teach: "wisdom" (knowing how to live skillfully), "discipline" (training in obeying God), "discretion" (choosing rightly between two ideas or two actions), and "prudence" (thinking through actions before you do them). God's wisdom rescues you from being simple or immature so you know how to act well toward yourself and others. It teaches you to wise up. It shows you where to go.

The incredible part is that the all-knowing God never

treats you like an idiot. He isn't like a professor parading his vastly superior knowledge.

But get this straight: *God can only teach you as much as you want to know.* You get smart only when you "fear God"—when you respectfully submit to His teaching because you know that you need Him to figure out life.

You'll always need to learn from the Father who knows best.

Through these proverbs, people will receive instruction in discipline, good conduct, and doing what is right, just, and fair. These proverbs will make the simpleminded clever. They will give knowledge and purpose to young people.

—PROVERBS 1:3–4 NLT

When you strike out on your own it's easy to feel like a tree stuck by your lonesome on the prairie, bent by the wind, scraggly for lack of water. You discover that no one ever lops a gushing hose at your roots. No one ever lovingly trims you to look like a giraffe or a flamingo. You might even teeter on the edge of insanity and wish you could plant yourself back in what you remember as the safe, protected greenhouse of high school.

And in your all-aloneness you might be tempted to conform to the swirl of new people and situations around you. You might worry you're going to lose your leaves, shrivel up, then tumble away in the wind if you don't.

Reality check: You're not the one who needs to worry about wilting. Here's what God promises His people: They drink from God's streams. They sprout fruit. They stand in God's presence. God watches over every detail of their lives (Psalm 1:1–3).

And here's what happens to those who distance themselves from God: They lack roots—no water, no food, no life. They're dried-out "chaff" (the husks left over from threshing wheat). They're blown away in the hurricane of God's judgment (Psalm 1:4–6).

It doesn't sound like you're missing much when you refuse to wallow with the wicked or saddle up with sinners or mesh with those who mock God.

*Happy are those who don't listen to the wicked, who
don't go where sinners go, who don't do
what evil people do.*

—PSALM 1:1 NCV

When you put God's kingdom and righteousness before all else, Jesus promised, all of your other concerns will fall into place.

To seek God's kingdom is to welcome God's reign in your life—to want what He wants. That's giving God your heart.

To seek God's righteousness is to look for ways to

love Him and others. That's giving God your life.

When you run hard and fast after God, He promises to take care of everything else: "All these things will be given to you as well."

That doesn't mean you never think about those other things. Birds dig worms and flowers drink, and it's not a bad idea for people to lay out clothes for the next day so they aren't late for school or work. But you don't need to huff yourself breathless figuring out what to buy or eat or play. You're running toward the wrong goal if you perpetually panic about what to wear without ever pondering how to live.

Your heavenly Father already knows all your needs, and he will give you all you need from day to day if you live for him and make the Kingdom of God your primary concern.
— MATTHEW 6:32–33 NLT

God respects you enough to make *you* ultimately responsible for yourself. He gives you parents and bosses and professors and other authorities to instruct and shape you. But in the end, you answer to God for yourself. Having authority over yourself is God's gift that allows you to follow Him not because you have to, but because you want to.

You abuse God's gift whenever you surrender control of yourself to anything or anyone other than Him. You might as well bind your hands, gag your mouth, and unplug your brain. If you don't control yourself, some other nasty thing will. A guy who lets friends tell him drugs are the ultimate trip has misplaced his brain. An unmarried girl who gets drunk and winds up in bed with a guy loses her body—and maybe her health or her life.

Letting your emotions or hormones run wild can destroy you. When you lose self-control, you're like an ancient city with broken-down walls. You have no protection. You have no power over who comes in or who goes out or what they do.

A person without self-control is as defenseless as a city with broken-down walls.

—PROVERBS 25:28 NLT

God is happy to guide you. In fact, He actually *invites* you to ask Him for direction: "If any of you lacks wisdom, he should ask God, who gives generously to all without finding fault, and it will be given to him" (James 1:5).

God never blames you for not knowing where to go in life. What He despises is "double-mindedness." He wants you to be sure of His care and sure that you intend to do what He says. If you waver between wanting what *God* wants and wanting to hear what *you* want, God isn't likely to give you the directions you're only sort-of asking for (James 1:6–7).

Asking God for guidance means you want to know

what God—in His absolute power and wisdom—thinks is best. And God almost always will lead you just one step at a time, checking your obedience and keeping you close to Him.

> *Patient endurance is what you need now, so you will continue to do God's will. Then you will receive all that he has promised.*
>
> —HEBREWS 10:36 NLT

God wants to show you where to go—but even so, your understanding of what He wants may be incomplete.

Picture this: You're driving on a country road on a moonless night. Your headlights brighten the road *one hundred* feet in front of you. But you're driving fast enough that even if you slammed on the brakes it would take *two hundred* feet to stop. You can't see as far ahead as you need to. You probably know that's called "overdriving your headlights." It's scary. You're cheesespread if a deer leaps in front of you or a curve comes up fast.

You probably want to drive your life with your foot to the floor. To push forward. For God to tell you exactly what your future holds and to get there fast.

But driving faster than God chooses to give you guidance is like plunging stupidly into the darkness.

Slow down. You won't ever waste your life if you live it God's way, at God's pace.

Wait for the Lord; be strong and take heart and wait for the Lord.

— PSALM 27:14

If you constantly asked a friend for directions to her house—but always took your own route and then complained about getting lost—she would give up trying to tell you the way. Likewise, God knows that unless you're ready to listen and obey, showing you truth is useless.

God enthusiastically gives wisdom to anyone who asks (James 1:5). He expects you to trust His desire and ability to answer your request. He expects you to believe Him enough to act on the truth He shows you—to follow His directions, to walk His way, to do what He says.

Faith trusts. Doubt hatches backup plans. It picks and chooses. Part of you wants God's truth, part of you doesn't. Part of you wants to obey, part of you won't.

Don't assume, though, that your faith has to be per-fect before God will answer you. No human being has perfect faith in God. What God wants to see is a faith that shouts, "I do believe. Help me believe more!" (Mark 9:24 NCV).

But when you ask him [for wisdom], be sure that you really expect him to answer, for a doubtful mind is as unsettled as a wave of the sea that is driven and tossed by the wind. People like that should not expect to receive anything from the Lord. They can't make up their minds.

—JAMES 1:6–8 NLT

LOCATING TRUE LOVE

PART TWO

PURITY, SEX, AND DATING

If you rate human experience from zero to ten, taking a bath with your hair dryer scores a definite zero—painful, scorching, and deadly. God intends sex to be *waaaaay* at the other end of the scale. But sex is only that great for those who wait.

God means for us to keep sexual intercourse—and the intense physical affection that precedes it—for marriage. Sex is God's wedding present to a man and a woman who seal their love through a public promise to stay together for life.

God's gift is hotter than a nuclear-powered toaster.

You don't want to power-up now. Locking lips starts a chain reaction God designed to end in an awesome explosion. If you feed fuel to the reactor *now*—in your thoughts, by what you watch and look at and listen to, by heated make-out extravaganzas, by the "goals" you set—you'll start a meltdown that sooner or later you won't stop.

The fire and fallout from breaking God's command are deadly. You worry about *conception*—creating a baby. Why gamble your future? You risk *infection*. Why risk death? You face *rejection* when the relationship ends. Why torment yourself? And you won't escape *detection*. Why strain your most important relationship—your friendship with God?

Marriage should be honored by everyone, and husband and wife should keep their marriage pure. God will judge as guilty those who take part in sexual sins.

—HEBREWS 13:4 NCV

What Jesus calls "lust" isn't mere curiosity about the opposite sex. It isn't wanting a really close friend—or even having a body that feels sexually hungry. Lust is grasping for *what* you can't have *when* you can't have it.

The Bible is clear that "adultery," sex outside of marriage, is wrong (Exodus 20:14; Hebrews 13:4). But Jesus says purity runs deeper than that. You don't have to roam under clothes or get pregnant to have gone "too far." Real purity is booting from your brain even *thoughts* of wrong things.

That's what Jesus means by His hyped-up language ("hyperbole") about getting rid of things that cause you to sin. If guys or girls gouged an eye every time their thoughts got hot, the ground would be littered with eyeballs. Everywhere you look and listen—magazines, TV, movies, software, jokes, videos, T-shirts, billboards—you're encouraged to let your thoughts wander to sex.

Here's the point: Jesus doesn't want you to mutilate yourself, but to cut off evil—to exit situations that tempt you (2 Timothy 2:22), look the other way when you need to (Job 31:1), and crowd out bad thoughts by filling your head with good ones (Philippians 4:6–8).

But I tell you that if anyone looks at a woman and wants to sin sexually with her, in his mind he has already done that sin with the woman. If your right eye causes you to sin, take it out and throw it away.

—MATTHEW 5:28–29 NCV

The toughest temptations you face nearly always have a face.

They have *cool* faces. You aren't tempted by a flea-infested drug dealer driving a beat-up car. A beautiful girl or a gorgeous guy is harder to resist.

They have *caring* faces. They laugh at your jokes. They make you feel good. They think you're brilliant. They understand how you think and feel. They spend time with you.

In order to stay friends with the people wearing those faces, you're tempted to do whatever they want. You might think about throwing out God's commands—ranking on the nearest nerd, joining in at the party, hooking up with a non-Christian, blowing off class or work, or blowing up at your parents. It feels right when you think those faces are cool and caring.

But coolness isn't a perfect complexion or clothes or a car. And caring isn't making you feel right when you're doing wrong. In a warped way pimps care for prostitutes and people care for their dogs. That doesn't mean you want to be a hooker or a hound.

Who's cool? Who cares for you? People who guide you into wisdom, watch to protect you, and remind you to stay on God's paths.

For these commands and this teaching are a lamp to light the way ahead of you. The correction of discipline is the way to life.

—PROVERBS 6:23 NLT

Sin is like two chains. Saying "yes" to God's offer of forgiveness in Jesus sets you free from one chain: the *penalty* of sin.

But there's a second chain: the *power* of sin. You maybe know about God's forgiveness. He also wants you to experience His freedom.

Sin hurts. But breaking that second chain starts with knowing you need to get free. When you know sin enchains you, you let God cut you loose.

You were taught to leave your old self—to stop living the evil way you lived before. That old self becomes worse, because people are fooled by the evil things they want to do.

—EPHESIANS 4:22 NCV

If purity were just about rules, you'd have reason to feel rotten. But it's better than that.

Yep, purity is about *performance—how you act*. It's about obedience and conforming to God's commands. But conforming isn't contorting—twisting yourself into a pretzel just because someone makes you.

Purity is also about *purpose—how you think and feel*. Jesus said that real purity starts with the heart (Matthew 5:21–22, 27–28). Not beating up an enemy is stupendous—but not if you're still stuffed full of hatred. Obeying those in authority is right on track—but you've derailed if you still steam on the inside. Saving sex for marriage is even better than best—but you're missing the point if you still allow lust into your mind and heart.

Get this: Purity is most of all about a *person—how you live close to Jesus*. It's no mystery. Purity isn't misery. Jesus said that anyone who serves Him follows Him (John 12:26). Real purity wants right stuff and sticks close to Jesus' side. It's true: The pure in heart see God.

God blesses those whose hearts are pure,
for they will see God.

—MATTHEW 5:8 NLT

When you get serious with someone of the opposite sex, you're a prisoner to love: You worry about what you say, what you wear, how you look. When you get labeled "boyfriend" or "girlfriend," you're best pals with some people and an instant enemy to others. If you talk to another guy or girl your beloved goes nuclear. And a guy-girl relationship is often like prison: When your sentence is up you're out. Your friendship often ends.

Few people are worth that. When you look back you're likely to wish you had a long-term friendship instead of a short-term relationship. So before you lock yourself up and eat the key, take a step back, go slow, and be friends first.

Friendship is the most important part of a guy-girl relationship. And Christ is the most important part of the most important part.

God says never to "yoke" yourself—which describes going together, dating, marriage, or even being best friends—with someone who isn't a Christian. You would be like animals clamped together straining to plow in different directions. You try to follow Christ, but where would they want to drag you?

So make your first goal finding a friend plowing toward Christ just as fast and hard as you.

Do not be yoked together with unbelievers. For what
do righteousness and wickedness have in common?
Or what fellowship can light have with darkness?
—2 CORINTHIANS 6:14

When you were little your parents could say, "That's a stove. It's hot. It will burn you." You might have said, "No, it's not." Or "No, it won't." But you were short enough that they had no problem putting you in your place to protect you.

Guess what? You're not so small anymore. And your parents' ability to keep your hands out of ovens and away from burners is pretty much gone.

Still, you've mastered the stove lesson. Your parents probably don't have to beat you back to keep you from broiling your fingers for breakfast. Why? At some point you decided your parents aren't stupid.

Most adults have done things they regret. What seemed fun at the time—and what might sound fun to you—doesn't look so good to them now. Like a whopper sunburn, the damage didn't show up until later. But they still got burned.

Your parents and other caring adults want you to learn from your mistakes—and from theirs. To do anything less is to be like a toddler too dumb to stay away from the stove—or like a dog that barfs once and eats twice. He goes back to chomp down what already made him sick, mistaking it for another meal.

A fool who repeats his foolishness is like a dog that goes back to what it has thrown up.

—PROVERBS 26:11 NCV

Blinded by a spotlight, cuffed like a criminal, wired to a lie detector—forced to be honest—none of us has a shortage of shortcomings. We know the rules well. Yet we fail to keep them perfectly—no matter how hard we try.

It's like an annoying hunk of hair that always curls the wrong way. Slick it down, mousse it up, as soon as you drop your guard: *fuh-wang!* Some of the curls in our character, though, aren't small. And they matter even more than doofy hair.

Even after we've decided to follow Jesus, sin still hounds us (Hebrews 12:1). Part of us wants to do what's right. Part of us doesn't. We can blame others, make excuses, or hide our faults, but it always comes back to one fact: there's something wrong with *us*. There's a war going on inside us.

But admitting we're a tangled mess opens the way for God to fix us. Being a Christian isn't just knowing the rules. It's not even knowing when you've broken them. It's relying on the Master to remake you.

Oh, what a miserable person I am! Who will free me from this life that is dominated by sin? Thank God! The answer is in Jesus Christ our Lord.

— ROMANS 7:24–25 NLT

FACTS IS FACTS

PART THREE

TRUTH, FAITH, AND WISDOM

God won't let the human race treat Him like a build-your-own tostada bar. You can't pick the guacamole but flick the onions, or choose the cheese but lose the beans, making God fit your taste. It's *never* okay to make God into what you think best—not to invent your own religion, nor to grab one from a group that creates gods and religions different from what the true God has revealed of himself in the Bible. God wants us to know Him exactly as He is—as He's shown himself to be.

Truth brings life. Lies bring death. Cults bring spiritual death to those who cling to their misshaped gods.

It's tempting to waffle on truth.

God won't.

It's easy to be tolerant, never speak bad, never say anyone is wrong about anything.

God is kind. But He isn't shy. He tells us that He alone is Truth (John 14:6).

Jesus is the only One who can save people. His name is the only power in the world that has been given to save people. We must be saved through him.

—ACTS 4:12 NCV

If you want to get unlost in life, the Bible is the place to look. It teaches you to know God and helps you mature. It shows you the way to real life.

Getting directions doesn't work if the directions you get aren't clear. But the Bible is "breathed by God" so that it provides perfect directions from the perfect God. If you look to God's Word—the Bible—for directions, you can trust what it says. It's your unique guidebook written by the ultimate guide, God himself.

All Scripture is inspired by God and is useful to teach us what is true and to make us realize what is wrong in our lives. It straightens us out and teaches us to do what is right.

— 2 TIMOTHY 3:16 NLT

When you go out to eat you never say, "Give me one of everything, please," then try to eat it all. You find out what's best and start there. So why try to gulp the Bible down all at once? If you're having a hard time reading the Bible regularly, start with a few of the Bible's choicest morsels, and later you can eat your way through the rest of the menu. Two of the easiest places to start are the Bible books of John—which will fill you in on Jesus' life—and Ephesians—which tells you who you are as a believer and how to live like one.

Food that you know tastes good will lure you closer. Jesus promises that He's that kind of food—food that satisfies better than anything else. *He* is what makes Bible reading something you do because you want to, not because you have to.

> *I am the living bread that came down from heaven.*
> *If anyone eats of this bread, he will live forever. This*
> *bread is my flesh, which I will give*
> *for the life of the world.*
>
> — JOHN 6:51

Truth can be hard to find. Peers fib behind your back and then to your face. Sports stars inflate their images to sell you the goods. Musicians and media distort, deceive, and mislead. Professors spout politically corrected "truth." Bosses pretend they want what's best for you just to get what's best for them.

And if you hadn't noticed, even people who *want* to be honest with you make mistakes. There's one fact you can be sure of: People don't always tell the truth.

Without God changing our minds and words, people naturally follow the "ruler of the kingdom of the air" (Ephesians 2:2), who is the "father of lies" (John 8:44). Truth gets lost and life becomes a sticky spider's web, a shadowy darkness, a confusing carnival.

It would be nice to think you could buy as true anything that people tell you. But don't plunk down your money until you understand how the game is played.

> *Your lips have spoken lies, and your tongue mutters*
> *wicked things. No one calls for justice; no one*
> *pleads his case with integrity. They rely on empty*
> *arguments and speak lies; they conceive trouble and*
> *give birth to evil.*
>
> — ISAIAH 59:3–4

You don't want to be *simple*—dim-witted, too stupid to watch where you're going. You don't want to be a *mocker*—sharp-tongued, too proud to accept advice. And you definitely don't want to be *foolish*—stubborn, too headstrong to be corrected, apt to repeat your mistakes.

The simple, the mockers, and the foolish have a few things in common. They like themselves just the way they are. They live as if God didn't exist. And catastrophe will liquidate them because they continually reject wisdom.

Not smart.

You won't straighten out every person in the world who rejects truth. But it *is* your job to be ready and able to explain, say, your faith—with gentleness and respect—to everyone who asks you to explain why you entrust your life to Christ (1 Peter 3:15).

And it's your job to not be duped when someone tries to sell you a different god—or no God—or rewritten rules of right and wrong. When you bump up against people who don't believe what you do, understand what they say. But understand, too, where they go wrong. After all, you can be so open-minded that your brain falls out.

Fools will die because they refuse to listen; they will be destroyed because they do not care. But those who listen to me will live in safety and be at peace, without fear of injury.

—PROVERBS 1:32–33 NCV

You can be unafraid of people who disagree with your beliefs because you accept the fact that Christ is Lord. After all, *Jesus* deserves your deepest awe and obedience. Your first concern should be what *He* thinks, not what others think. Besides, if you can stop your fears from ringing in your ears, you'll be able to hear the Holy Spirit help you know what to say and when to speak (Mark 13:11).

If you want to demonstrate to others that God is real, nothing beats real love, the example of a changed life, and simple sharing. God isn't looking for loud de- bates with your bosses or teachers or classmates. He doesn't require a big show but a pure heart—"a clear conscience" that silences lies people say about you.

After this prayer, the building where they were meeting shook, and they were all filled with the Holy Spirit. And they preached God's message with boldness.

—ACTS 4:31 NLT

On loads of college campuses, cults genuinely endanger your faith. What cults teach, spiritually speaking, is an eternal enchilada short of a Tex-Mex combo. Get ahold of this blunt truth: Their message of how to know God leads people away from true saving faith. To a savior other than Jesus. In the other direction from heaven. What might seem like a *what's the big deal?* issue to us actually decides whether someone is in the kingdom or not. For now. And forever.

Your faith needs to be clear and strong so that you don't land in a cult. But just as important, your faith needs to be powerful enough to avoid getting between belief systems. A cult *might* not persuade you to follow their faith, but they might be one of many forces in life that wears you down and convinces you to chuck your faith and thumb a big "Who Needs It!" at Christianity, convinced that no one has the real truth about God.

You don't want to get sucked in.

You don't want to get stuck.

> *Be on guard. Stand true to what you believe. Be courageous. Be strong. And everything you do must be done with love.*
> — 1 CORINTHIANS 16:13–14 NLT

When people play games with truth, the world grinds to a halt. When people lie to you, it's hard to know what to believe or whom to trust, who's a winner or who's a loser, who deserves a reward or who deserves punishment, what's good or what's bad, who your friends are or who wants to hurt you.

You don't like being lied to, so don't lie to others. That's what the Bible means when it says, "Speak truth, because you are members of one body." Truth is so important to the way the world works that God lumps lying with sins most people would never do—like murder, satanism, and idolatry (Revelation 22:15).

Playing keep-away with the truth never wins.

So you must stop telling lies. Tell each other the truth, because we all belong to each other in the same body.

—EPHESIANS 4:25 NCV

Words aren't worth trusting if they aren't backed up by actions. From the Bible's point of view, truth is more than promises or bare facts or correct thoughts. Truth is something that is *lived*. Without love, words are worthless (1 John 4:18).

Truth without love is like poison in a Popsicle: sweet but deadly.

Scripture is the first test of truth. Love is the second. People worth trusting aren't necessarily the ones who know the most, but rather the ones who combine knowledge with real-life love. People who love as God loves are the ones who have grasped truth.

You can't escape people whose brains are bigger than their hearts, but you can avoid being duped by them. If your parents habitually make ungodly choices, you might need to pick a role model other than your folks. If a teacher you like wanders away from God's truth, at times you'll need to study up on a point of view other than your teacher's. And if a friend makes you doubt what you believe, you'll have to decide whether that's the kind of friend you can listen to.

If I knew all the mysteries of the future and knew everything about everything, but didn't love others, what good would I be?

— 1 CORINTHIANS 13:2 NLT

WHO GOD IS AND WHAT GOD'S DONE

PART FOUR

LOVE, GRACE, AND SALVATION

One second the Son of God was ruling the universe with the Father and Holy Spirit in the dazzling brightness of heaven. The next second He was born on earth—still totally God, but now also fully human. Angels proclaimed who He was: Savior, Messiah, Lord. He was called Immanuel ("God with us") and Jesus ("the Lord saves") (Matthew 1:21–23). Think of it! God came to visit His creation.

God saw that His critically injured world needed help. He didn't just gaze at us from a distance, where problems disappear in a haze. He came as a friend—in the flesh, right here. See, God knew that real friends don't just send sympathy cards. They show up in person.

And when He came to visit, He did more than sit in a chair next to our bed and pity us. By leaving His glory and coming to earth, He, too, climbed into a body cast just like us, so we can be certain He knows what we go through (Hebrews 4:14–16). He felt the same temptations and limitations we do. He felt the craziness of itching where you can't scratch beneath a cast. He didn't leave us suffering alone.

But the angel said to them, "Do not be afraid. I bring you good news of great joy that will be for all the people. Today in the town of David a Savior has been born to you; he is Christ the Lord."

—LUKE 2:10–11

Christians mess up. Plenty. God promises, though, that if we admit our sins He will forgive us and make us clean again (1 John 1:8–9). He gives our relationship a fresh start each and every time.

Even though Jesus has made you once-and-for-all right with God—and even though confessing sin and trusting God's forgiveness lets you enjoy God's gracious friendship—Satan wants you to still feel guilty. To act like you have something to hide. To avoid God's eyes and run away when you hear Him coming. Satan retains enough authority on earth and status in heaven to go before God and shriek that you're still guilty, and his accusations ring in your ears back on earth.

Satan's twisted tongue is so much a part of who he is and how he acts in the world that Jesus called him "a liar and the father of lies" (John 8:44).

Want to plug your ears? Cling to God's promises of forgiveness through Christ's blood shed for you (Revelation 12:10–11).

Let us come boldly to the throne of our gracious God. There we will receive his mercy, and we will find grace to help us when we need it.

— HEBREWS 4:16

Asking most people how to get into a relationship with God isn't much help. They're lost too. "Look for God inside yourself," they say. "Work hard to be good enough for God. Trust cold concrete data and nothing else. Accept fate. Make up your own beliefs. Look to spirits and stars. Pummel your body to perfection. Get rid of desire—care about nothing."

Human thought can't lead you through life to an eternity of paradise with God. Its destinations are confused. Its routes are dead ends.

Jesus knows where you really need to go. He knows how to get there. He's tracked you down. He says, "I am the way and the truth and the life. Want to come home?" Only Jesus is the Way—He died for you and opened the gate back to God. Only Jesus is the Truth—He gives a perfect picture of God. Only Jesus is the Life—He conquers death so you can live eternally.

He's the one road to where you belong.

Jesus answered, "I am the way and the truth and the life. No one comes to the Father except through me."

— J O H N   1 4 : 6

Each time we disobey—when we sin by what we think, say, or do—we lay a brick between ourselves and God. He doesn't build the wall. *We* do each time we choose to sin. Sin separates us from God as we build that wall brick by brick. Sin makes it impossible for us to be God's friends.

Separation is also God's final punishment for wrongdoing. If we refuse God's way of demolishing the wall, we will discover that when we die, the wall cements for eternity (Romans 6:23). We'll find ourselves cut off from God and *everything* good He has made. No phone, TV, radio, or satellite dish will tie us to family or friends or God on the other side of the wall. Being cemented inside the wall—in hell—isn't a fairy tale. It's real.

Yet if you read in Luke 15, you'll find the story of a son who came home to his waiting, love-sick father. Our Father in heaven is waiting for us too, so that *we* can be friends again with Him. To make this possible, God sent His son, Jesus Christ, to tear down the wall we have built. We just need to come home.

> *While he was still a long way off, his father saw him and was filled with compassion for him; he ran to his son, threw his arms around him and kissed him. The son said to him, "Father, I have sinned against heaven and against you. I am no longer worthy to be called your son."*
>
> —LUKE 15:20–21

God promises to adopt all who say yes to Him.

Christ's death and resurrection is God's offer to adopt you. And the offer is free, no strings attached. Our sins made us God's enemies, but Christ's death made it possible for us to be His friends (Colossians 1:21–23).

If you've never been a part of God's family or grown

up taking your heavenly Father for granted, you can say to God, "Because I've done wrong, I need you. I believe that Christ died for my sins. I accept your for-giving love. I want to be your child." That's how you become a Christian. That's how you become one of His people.

In God's family, everyone is adopted.

It's the only way in.

To all who did accept him and believe in him he gave the right to become children of God.

— JOHN 1:12 NCV

In Christ, God acted to rescue you. Christ died to bring forgiveness and a life close to God. But you won't ever feel freedom if you don't believe Him and act on what you believe.

Grab hold of what He's done for you:

- If you believe that God has forgiven and accepted you, then talk to Him confidently (Hebrews 10:19–22).

- If you're sure God protects you, then fear nothing (Psalm 118:6).

- If you know that hardship is God's discipline, then resolve to learn from what you can't change (Hebrews 12:11).

- If you accept God's love for you, then love others (1 John 4:19).

- If you trust that God wants what's best for you, then obey (Psalm 19:7–11).

If you don't act on good news, it can't change your life.

Then the Lord said to Moses, "Why are you crying out to me? Tell the people to get moving!"

— EXODUS 14:15 NLT

John Newton was twenty-two when he became the master of a slave ship. What a wretched guy—evil beyond words! Shuttling men, women, and children in chains, he treated and traded people like pigs. Surely Newton deserved to be voted *Least Likely to Become a Decent Guy.* But Newton became a Christian. He worked to abolish slavery. And later he wrote these words:

> *Amazing grace, how sweet the sound,*
> *That saved a wretch like me.*
> *I once was lost, but now am found,*
> *Was blind, but now I see.*

Newton discovered that Christ's death was big and bold enough to pay for sins even as enormous as his. God's grace scrubbed even a slave trader clean. He must have banged his forehead and said, "Wow! I've been forgiven!"

Grace should amaze you. Every good thing you have, are, or do is given to you by grace. God forgives you. He loves you. Every day of life. No matter what mess you're in. Grace is also what grows you. It teaches you "to deny ungodliness and worldly desires and to live sensibly, righteously and godly in the present age" (Titus 2:12 NASB).

God saved you by his special favor when you
believed. And you can't take credit for this; it is a
gift from God. Salvation is not a reward
for the good things we have done,
so none of us can boast about it.

— EPHESIANS 2:8–9 NLT

When you've been at war with God, the one right response to Him is to accept His terms of truce—to trust in who Jesus is and what He accomplished for us. These are the terms of the friendship He offers: "To all who received him, to those who believed in his name, he gave the right to become children of God" (John 1:12).

To receive Him means we change our minds about sin. God doesn't want us just to be sad that His cosmic X-ray vision spotted us sneaky little evildoers. He doesn't want us sorry we got caught but sorry for the hurt our rebellion has caused ourselves, others, and Him. And aware of the wrongness of our wrong.

To receive Him means we change our minds about God. We finally admit that God's commands are wholly good, totally kind. That Jesus is God in a bod. That His gift of forgiveness is the one way our sins can be wiped away so we can be accepted by Him.

Receiving Him might be an attitude of trust and faith that grows over time. Or receiving Christ might happen in a prayer you can pinpoint in time and space— one you can pray right now: "God, I know I've sinned against you. Thank you that Christ died in my place and took the punishment I deserved. Thank you for forgiving me. Help me to follow you." Either way, the result is the same: You start a new life as God's friend.

For if you confess with your mouth that Jesus is
Lord and believe in your heart that God raised him
from the dead, you will be saved.

—ROMANS 10:9 NLT

THE REAL AND THE FAKE

PART FIVE

GOD'S WAY
VS.
THE HUMAN WAY

You don't live in this world by yourself. You bump people. They shove you. They stretch you. And sometimes they gang up and squish you. That's peer pressure.

So? You've heard that before. Parents, teachers, and tacky TV commercials have been telling you since you were two that peers can mislead and crush you.

But the big surprise might be that peers don't stop influencing you when you exit high school. With all those new friends you make when you move out on your own, you inevitably get molded into a new shape.

Now, peer pressure isn't all bad. If it weren't for peer fear you'd still pick your nose in public. Deep down you know you can't live isolated from your peers, and a lot of times it's fine to want to fit in. Isn't a true nerd, after all, someone who lives in his or her own wee little world, clueless of when and how it's *okay* or even good to conform?

Yet you can never be all your peers want you to be. Paul pointed out one area—your faith as a Christian— where it's never right to settle for being shaped by the forces that surround you. The facts that Christ died and rose for you, forgives you, and deserves total obedience to His commands aren't ideas you can re-define or redesign. They aren't open for negotiation. You don't swap them to win points with people.

Sometimes you can act, talk, dress, and think in a way that is seen as wonderful by both God and the people around you (2 Corinthians 8:21; Hebrews

12:14). Other times you can't. It's a choice. But it's no contest whose opinion matters more (Luke 12:4–5).

Do you think I am trying to make people accept me? No, God is the One I am trying to please. Am I trying to please people? If I still wanted to please people, I would not be a servant of Christ.

— GALATIANS 1:10 NCV

What would Jesus look like if He came to the world today?

You wouldn't expect Him to be born in a stable or grow up to be a carpenter—a sweaty construction worker. If we had our way, we'd remake Jesus into a president, a movie star, and a superathlete rolled into one.

He'd only sweat with His personal trainer. He'd ditch the beard and maybe get a goatee. He'd need makeup, hair that doesn't flinch in a tornado, and antiperspirant strong enough to keep a gorilla dry under stage lights. And He'd wear sandals only where it was environmentally correct—in the Pacific North-west (up in the mountains) and in small pockets of enviro-hip Los Angeles.

He'd get wired with a little speaker in His ear so His handlers could tell Him what to say. When He spoke He'd have no awkward moments, no lapses in smoothness. He'd offend no one.

He'd stay out of small towns and away from children.

The only stops on His world tour would be 60,000-seat stadiums in cities bigger than a million people. When He went out in public He'd be surrounded by bodyguards with antennas in their hats and Uzi burp guns under their suit coats.

And if everything was planned just right, Jesus would be on TV no matter where you flipped. A billion-dollar ad blitz and a swarm of reporters tracking Jesus could make Him seem omnipresent—like He was everywhere all the time.

Those are the things that wow us. They get our attention.

But Jesus wasn't any of those things we think He should be.

"For my thoughts are not your thoughts, neither are your ways my ways," declares the Lord. "As the heavens are higher than the earth, so are my ways higher than your ways and my thoughts than your thoughts."

—ISAIAH 55:8–9

Big and powerful people can make you do what they say. You might not be a fan, but you're *forced* to follow.

Other people don't need to *make* you like them. You enjoy them because they make you laugh. Or you cheer for them when they dash around like superheroes in masks and tights crushing evildoers. Or you swoon when you see them because you dream of singing—or shooting hoops—or skiing—or skating—the way they do. They're too cool to contain your enthusiasm.

You don't sit down and decide who your heroes will be. You hear what others say, see who looks the prettiest, watch who scores the most. You don't use a checklist.

Maybe you should.

Paul listed all the reasons why Timothy should imitate him and heed what he said (2 Timothy 3:10–11). Paul was real. He didn't set a record, get rich, get high, and kill himself six months later. His coolness lasted a lifetime, through victories and catastrophes.

Most pop heroes turn out to be wax figures who melt in the heat. It's usually the heroes close-by—like parents, grandparents, teachers, pastors, youth counselors—who turn out to be eternal stars.

But you must remain faithful to the things you have been taught. You know they are true, for you know you can trust those who taught you.

— 2 TIMOTHY 3:14 NLT

This world has chosen to run from God. So if you're trying to run *toward* Him you're going to bang heads with people going the other way. Big things, little things. You won't always fit perfectly with your peers.

The problem isn't what your parents taught you or how they raised you—they want what's best for you. It isn't God—what He commands is always good. It isn't you—provided you're trying to do what's right. It isn't even the people around you. It's bigger than that.

The real problem is that this planet isn't your home. As a Christian you're a citizen of heaven (Philippians 3:20). And that makes you an "alien" and "stranger" here.

When you follow God you always ache for something better. But it isn't until heaven that you receive *all* that God has promised: A room in God's mansion (John 14:2). A spot in the city of God, where there's no more crying or pain (Revelation 21:3–4). A forever family where no one will argue about what's wrong and right (Hebrews 8:11).

It's where you belong.

It's a long walk before you get there.

But it's the one place where you'll feel totally at home.

Great people died in faith. . . . They said they were
like visitors and strangers on earth. They were
waiting for a better country—a heavenly country. So
God is not ashamed to be called their God, because
he has prepared a city for them.

—HEBREWS 11:13, 16 NCV

A human being who rules a country with total control is called an "absolute monarch" or a "dictator." No human being has the right or the ability to handle that much power.

God does. God is no human being. He *is* ruler of all. He made everything and has complete authority over it (Psalm 24:1–2). That would be unbearable if God's love for us weren't perfect. But it is, so He's worthy of our total devotion.

Yet not everyone agrees. The Bible talks in a hazy way about the beginning of a rebellion against God. Satan, whom God had made the most beautiful of all created beings (Ezekiel 28:12–19), decided *he* should be in charge. He believed he was wiser than God.

Satan puts our fears about God into words. He spends his time trying to persuade the world that *he*, not God, is the one worth listening to.

He's wrong.

For you said to yourself, "I will ascend to heaven and set my throne above God's stars. I will preside on the mountain of the gods far away in the north. I will climb to the highest heavens and be like the Most High." But instead, you will be brought down to the place of the dead, down to its lowest depths.

—ISAIAH 14:13–15 NLT

When someone mistreats you—slugs you or

pranks you or stabs you in the back—the Bible urges you to respond in a way you wouldn't expect. Your first responsibility is to "do what is right" and "live at peace with everyone." Rather than getting even, you're to fix the situation peacefully. The person you're battling with might make peace impossible, but you shouldn't.

"The best way to get rid of an enemy," wrote F. F. Bruce, "is to turn him into a friend." If you want to get back at someone and really mess up his mind, love him. Help him. Be kind to him. That's the only hope you have of disarming him and getting him on your side.

My friends, do not try to punish others when they wrong you, but wait for God to punish them with his anger. It is written: "I will punish those who do wrong; I will repay them," says the Lord.

—ROMANS 12:19

Jesus had a way of letting what people said slide right off.

Jesus didn't return the insults flung at Him—that would make Him as bad as His tormentors. Instead, He trusted the Father, who sees perfectly. He realized God's opinion counted more than all of the others put together.

Ponder this: Do the people who shred you know you? Not as well as God does. Is what people say true? If there actually is something wrong with you, God tells you constructively—with great timing, gently, helping you change.

Next time someone insults you, let it slip off by listening to what God says about you. You're His daughter or son. He loves you more than anyone else does. Listen for *God's* evaluation of your words, dress, looks, attitudes, actions, sins, faults, and skills. It's God's opinion that counts.

He [Jesus] did not retaliate when he was insulted.
When he suffered, he did not threaten to get even.
He left his case in the hands of God,
who always judges fairly.
—1 PETER 2:23 NLT

Christian speaker Tony Campolo is famous for asking if a Christian can own a BMW. Here's a different angle: Why do you want to? Aren't there more important things in life? As you become an adult it's easy to misplace your head. You see all the possibilities: a big house filled with neat stuff, a hot car, a cushy life. Amid the glitz you forget God's goal for the world. (To be fair, you can also get stuck on being poor. You can be so frugal and so intent on saving money that you also push aside God's plan as well.)

When you're learning how to make a living, learn balance. Listen to this proverb: "Give me neither poverty nor riches, but give me only my daily bread. Otherwise, I may have too much and disown you and say,

'Who is the Lord?' Or I may become poor and steal, and so dishonor the name of my God" (Proverbs 30:8–9). Keeping your head screwed on means you learn to be content with what you have because God and His purposes for you come first.

I have learned how to get along happily whether I have much or little. I know how to live on almost nothing or with everything. I have learned the secret of living in every situation, whether it is with a full stomach or empty, with plenty or little. For I can do everything with the help of Christ who gives me the strength I need.

— PHILIPPIANS 4:11–13 NLT

WE GOTTA GIVE IT ALL

PART SIX

DISCIPLESHIP,
ATTITUDE,
AND
CHRISTLIKENESS

What would you say if someone asked you why you're here on Planet Earth? Are you here just to consume oxygen? To master video games? To inhale the contents of your parents' refrigerator or the school snack bar—excluding the vegetable drawer? To rule the world?

Think bigger.

You're here to live like Christ. You're destined to do the things He did (Ephesians 2:10). You're here, in short, to be a servant like your Master. But what does *that* look like?

Jesus tried to tell His disciples that He would suffer and die. They didn't get it. They thought that to be Jesus—God's Son—was to rule the world and crush the opposition. They thought that to be His follower was to rule with Him and squish people they detested. They didn't understand that being like Him meant serving like Him.

Jesus-style servanthood isn't made up of acts like helping old ladies across the street. It's a way of life, caring even for "insignificant" people—like little kids, your enemies, "losers," people you know, and people you don't. It's learning to show love to everyone around you.

Jesus sat down and called the twelve apostles to him.
He said, "Whoever wants to be the most important
must be last of all and servant of all."

—MARK 9:35 NCV

People usually become slaves because they have no choice. In Bible times people sold themselves or their children to pay back money they owed. Not long ago Africans were brutalized and forced to serve against their wills.

But Exodus 21 shows a slave who said no to freedom so he could stay with his master. His master took the slave to a doorpost and pierced the slave's ear. (Don't try that at home—unless your mom is in to distressed-look woodwork.) Piercing an ear showed that the slave was forever a "bondservant," someone who serves a master because he *wants* to.

Crazy? The bondservant didn't think so. He wanted to work hard for his master because he was thankful for what the master had given him—security, love, a family, food, a home.

Paul often called himself a bondservant of Jesus Christ (see Romans 1:1). Paul was so sure of God's love that he chose to obey God in every way he knew. Unlike human masters, God is a righteous and good master. God gives us "every good and perfect gift" (James 1:17), from life itself to His never-ending love.

God doesn't twist your arm to make you serve Him. He isn't a slave master who beats you into submission. He earns your respect, trust, and love. Once you're sure that God loves you and wants the best for you, then it's not so crazy—or so hard—to love Him back.

> *The slave may plainly declare, "I love my master,*
> *my wife, and my children. I would rather not go*
> *free." If he does this, his master must present him*
> *before God. Then his master must take him to the*
> *door and publicly pierce his ear with an awl. After*
> *that, the slave will belong to his master forever.*
>
> —EXODUS 21:5–6 NLT

Face it. You're not perfect. Neither is anyone else.

But despite your failings, God doesn't put you and the rest of your species on display in a zoo built for losers. He sees something special in you, because He made you (Psalm 100:3). Nothing can separate you from His love (Romans 8:38–39), which reaches to the heavens (Psalm 36:5). And don't forget this: God's colossal love for you and your fellow earthlings is why He sent his Son, Jesus, to live and die (John 3:16).

News flash: When you know God loves you, you love others. If God had wanted you to make pets of the less-than-likable people around you, He would have built them with collars. Seeing none, it's obvious He wants you to do more than collect nerds. He wants you to love them with the love He lavishes on you.

> *We love each other as a result of his loving us first.*
>
> —1 JOHN 4:19 NLT

First great thing about doing good: If you do

right, you have nothing to fear (Romans 13:3). That beats being afraid of getting in trouble.

Second great thing about doing good: When you hunger for God and His ways, God fills you up so you can be wildly happy doing what's best. When you really want righteousness—right attitudes and actions, inside and out—He remakes you to want to be good not only for your own sake but also for the world around you to work right.

And when you want God's right thing in God's right time, He'll give it to you.

Take delight in the Lord, and he will
give you your heart's desires.

—PSALM 37:4 NLT

Non-Christians don't need our bumper stickers or T-shirts.

They're looking for God's good stuff inside us.

How we vote won't transmogrify the world—though voting is swell. We're not distinguished by our health or wealth—in fact, we search for better riches. And we don't rub our goodness in people's faces—that isn't what Jesus meant by being "a city set on a hill."

If you want to be happy, do good, make friends, and show off God, check out what Jesus said in Matthew 5:3–12 and Matthew 6:1–6. Jesus gave you the list of the 'tudes he's building in you.

You are the light of the world. A city on a hill cannot be hidden. . . . Let your light shine before men, that they may see your good deeds and praise your Father in heaven.

—MATTHEW 5:14, 16

Jesus doesn't just muscle your obedience. His total goodness deserves your respect. He's what the Bible calls "worthy."

He's worthy of your praise because He saves you from your enemies (2 Samuel 22:4). Because He is to be "feared above all gods" (1 Chronicles 16:25). Because His greatness is beyond imagination (Psalm 145:3).

In Revelation, the twenty-four elders surround the throne of God to shout, "You are worthy, our Lord and God, to receive glory and honor and power, for you created all things, and by your will they were created and have their being" (Revelation 4:11). Jesus is worthy of *glory*—wearing the shining majesty of God's presence. *Honor*—receiving respect that reaches to the stars. And *power*—wielding unlimited might and authority.

You can't give Him those things. He already has them as unfailing parts of His being. But you can recognize them. You can shout to Jesus, "YOU DA MAN!" Except it's "YOU THE GOD OF ALL!"

> Then I heard every creature in heaven and on earth
> and under the earth and on the sea, and all that is
> in them, singing: "To him who sits on the throne
> and to the Lamb be praise and honor and glory and
> power, for ever and ever!"
>
> — REVELATION 5:13

Quitting a job or a team or an activity doesn't always mean you're a quitter. You need to quit when you're hurting yourself—when you can't get enough sleep, you cry your eyes out nightly, or you don't get your homework done. You don't have much choice but to quit when you're forced to do wrong—by a crooked boss, for example. And it's okay to quit when you can do better at something else, *after* you've stuck it out and kept your promises. Commitments you made first—not the ones you like best—come first. Get help while you sweat it out, even if that means someone else takes some of your jobs.

> Dear brothers and sisters, whenever trouble comes
> your way, let it be an opportunity for joy.
> For when your faith is tested,
> your endurance has a chance to grow.
>
> — JAMES 1:2-3 NLT

If you belong to God, it changes how you treat people.

Love is the big test of whether or not you know God
(1 John 4:7–8). This is one test that covers real problems, checking whether you let God's love for you
reach through you to others. Words not backed by
actions are like not coloring in the whole circle on a
standardized test. They don't score, because love is
only love when it's demonstrated in real life.

You get chances every day to love in unshowy ways—
chances to be kind, to encourage, to admit you're
wrong, or to halt jealousy, lust, anger, and selfishness.

We know what real love is because Christ gave up
his life for us. And so we also ought to give up our
lives for our Christian friends. Dear children, let us
stop just saying we love each other; let us really
show it by our actions.

— 1 JOHN 3:16, 18 NLT

When you get out on your own you won't likely
have anyone dragging you out of bed to worship ser-
vices, to Bible study, or scads of other opportunities
for spiritual growth. And why go if no one is goading
you from behind?

God is all-powerful: Lord, Master, Judge. God is all-
kind: the Giver of forgiveness through Christ. But if
you don't perceive God's mind-boggling perfection,
then making the effort to grow closer to God doesn't
make sense. Being a Christian becomes rules and rit-
ual—just the right thing to do—rather than a relationship with your God.

God himself is the reason behind everything you do as a Christian. And church is your prime place to get close to God and God's people. Your *mouth* worships. You tell God how great He is. You "shout aloud to the Rock," the one who rescues you from sin's power and penalty. No mumbling meaningless words, though—your *heart* worships too. You acknowledge that you belong to God. You agree that His will is good. And you worship with your *life*, giving yourself to Him out of thankfulness for what He's done for you (Romans 12:1).

God doesn't drag you to church. He wants you to grasp His greatness.

Come, let us bow down in worship, let us kneel
before the Lord our Maker; for he is our God and we
are the people of his pasture,
the flock under his care.

— PSALM 95:6–7

THE ULTIMATE FRIEND

PART SEVEN

PRAYER,
TRUST,
AND
GOD'S WILL

Being a Christian won't plop you into a calm sea tickled by a gentle breeze. It might stir up storms. And Jesus' daring invitation sounds even crazier than rowing across a stormy lake or walking on water: *Know me*, He says. *Live for me*.

But Jesus *never* leaves you to face the winds alone. He's at your house when your family fights or you can't get along with your roommate. He's standing with you and your friends when you have to make gigantic choices. He's next to you when you find out a classmate killed himself or a girl you know well gets pregnant.

When darkness upsets your sense of direction, when winds scream and spray pokes your eyes, Jesus comes to you and says, "I'm not a ghost or a fantasy or too good to be true. I'm real. Don't be afraid! It's me! I'm here!"

Jesus is worth trusting. Not because He makes your sea smooth and your sky full of poofy marshmallow clouds—life doesn't always happen that way. He's worth your life because He's God's Son, who died and rose to stomp across waves with you, all because He loves you.

Instantly Jesus reached out his hand and grabbed him. "You don't have much faith," Jesus said. "Why did you doubt me?" And when they climbed back into the boat, the wind stopped. Then the disciples worshiped him. "You really are the Son of God!" they exclaimed.

—MATTHEW 14:31–33 NLT

How long until you show up? the Bible's King David prayed at God. *Remember me? Or have you forgotten who I am and what I need?* Those are pretty harsh words from the mouth of the guy Scripture applauds as "a man after God's own heart" (1 Samuel 13:14). But David spoke his mind and lived to tell about it.

Big feelings simmer inside when you have confused thoughts or painful emotions or a hurting body. Sometimes harsh words boil over onto yourself, people around you, even God—*especially* toward God, the one with ultimate power and complete control.

You don't have to hide your pain. David wasn't afraid to tell God about his hurts. They were real. But he always got around to thinking about a bigger reality—that God's love never quits. David didn't stop at speaking his mind and his heart. He spouted until he was able to praise God again.

> *How long will you forget me, Lord? Forever? How long will you hide from me? How long must I worry and feel sad in my heart all day? How long will my enemy win over me?*
>
> —PSALM 13:1-2 NCV

You can spend time with God two ways: in a group or by yourself. You need both to grow spiritually. In a group you're encouraged by the strong faith and support of other Christians. Groups allow you to get fired up and celebrate your friendship with God.

Getting alone to be with God helps you get to know

Him personally, just like you need time one-on-one with someone to really know that person. That's what Jesus did. Even He needed time to talk with God alone.

Very early in the morning, while it was still dark, Jesus got up, left the house and went off to a solitary place, where he prayed.

—MARK 1:35

Members of the Flat Earth Society want you

to believe—*surprise*—that the earth is flat. From observations you make in everyday life, it's tough to disagree with them. One glance outside should cause you to say, "Yup. Flat like a pancake."

But as soon as you get a bigger view—like the pictures of the earth astronauts take from space—you're forced to say, "Nope. Round like a ball."

We have to admit that we don't have complete understanding of ourselves and our world. It's God who has the big picture: a view of all people and all events for all time.

Jesus said His teaching wasn't something He made up on His own. He spoke as God's Son, who came "from above," from the Father in heaven. He repeated what He heard from His Father. He warned us for our own good, so we could go back with Him to heaven (John 14:2–4).

Confusing? The crowds around Jesus thought so. But

the point is that Jesus didn't speak as an ordinary human. He saw more than we do. And He knows more than we do.

> *Then he [Jesus] said to them, "You are from below; I*
> *am from above. You are of this world; I am not.*
> *That is why I said that you will die in your sins; for*
> *unless you believe that I am who I say I am, you*
> *will die in your sins."*
>
> —JOHN 8:23–24 NLT

Have you or a friend ever prayed and it seemed God didn't hear? You prayed for your parents—they still got divorced. You prayed for your grandparents—they got sick and died. You prayed for a scholarship—and it didn't show up. Or you prayed for smaller things—like good grades, a place on the team, a role in a play—and nothing seemed to happen.

Even the big believers of the Bible had experiences like that. Paul, for example, had an excruciating problem, probably an illness. But prayer didn't change Paul's circumstances. It changed Paul.

When you don't see the answers you want to your prayers, try to see what God is working to develop in you and in your relationship with Him. Prayer *always* changes the person who prays in faith *if* he or she trusts that God hears and cares. Prayer that seems to fail produces a Christian who succeeds.

> *I begged the Lord three times to take this problem*
> *away from me. But he said to me, "My grace is*
> *enough for you. When you are weak, my power is*
> *made perfect in you."*
>
> —2 CORINTHIANS 12:8–9 NCV

No circumstance of your life outsmarts God's control. He can rearrange pain or remove it—but if He doesn't shoo away the troubles that tromp through your life, count those troubles as part of God's training to make you like Him.

Pain only works its wonders if you submit to its training. When you accept as part of God's discipline the hardships that strike out of nowhere and slap you upside the head, He makes them into something useful. They'll make you righteous and peaceful. And they'll remind you that you're truly God's daughter or son.

If you try to wiggle free from the weights in God's gym, though, what's supposed to be your spiritual workout is a waste—it just wastes *you*, that is. It becomes stupid suffering, not a sweaty workout for your soul.

If you understand that tough times are God's discipline, you'll learn from what you can't change.

> *My child, do not reject the Lord's discipline, and*
> *don't get angry when he corrects you. The Lord*
> *corrects those he loves, just as parents correct the*
> *child they delight in.*
>
> —PROVERBS 3:11–12 NCV

It's no surprise when enemies lie about you, talk behind your back, leave you in the dust, or punch you in the stomach.

It's harder to understand when friends do those things. You do your best to be a good friend, you work out conflicts, you love like Christ loves—and a friendship still blows up in your face. Sooner or later it happens to everyone. You moan and groan with hurt and feel like a reject.

Yet if you trust God to get you through the hurt, you'll survive. God can make it okay to be alone, because *He's* still your friend. He sees what you need in the darkness or behind slammed doors—even inside your head or on a page of your diary.

When you have God as your friend, pain is only part of what you write in a diary or journal, only part of what you think and feel. The last line you write—or the thought to focus on through an awful, lonely day—can always be, "God, I trust you. I belong to you. Help me."

> *For the eyes of the Lord range throughout the earth*
> *to strengthen those whose hearts*
> *are fully committed to him.*
>
> —2 CHRONICLES 16:9a

Imposters offer cruel dictatorship. Jesus offers righteous Lordship.

Jesus is the one Being capable of running the universe. He's the right God for the job. He's the one real God. He's the only one fit to look after our lives. He's the only one who has died and risen to give us spiritual life. Life with Him—friendship with the worthy one—is the only thing that can satisfy us.

God invites you to give yourself willingly. Submit to Him gladly.

> *And they all sang a new song to the Lamb: "You*
> *are worthy to take the scroll and to open its seals,*
> *because you were killed, and with the blood of your*
> *death you bought people for God from every tribe,*
> *language, people, and nation."*
>
> —REVELATION 5:9 NCV

Sheep know their shepherd treats them right. He gives each a name. He provides for their needs—food during the day, shelter at night. The shepherd stands at the gate of the pen to check the sheep one by one, soothing wounds and providing security. The sheep know their shepherd's unique call and scatter at anyone else's voice.

By experiencing the shepherd's kindness, the sheep know that their shepherd isn't like others who sneak into the pen and hurt them. The shepherd's one concern is the good of those in his care.

Once you know that Jesus' main concern is to lead you into the best life God has in mind for you, then you won't be fooled by violent or stealthy voices that want to turn you into lamb chop. You know they don't sound like Jesus. Jesus' voice is kind. Jesus is your Good Shepherd.

"The thief comes only to steal and kill and destroy; I have come that they may have life, and have it to the full. I am the good shepherd. The good shepherd lays down his life for the sheep."

— JOHN 10:10–11

Just because you *want* to do what's right doesn't mean you will always *know* what's right. In the Bible God makes clear ninety-nine percent of what He wants you to do—and not do. But when it comes to showing you your future, He usually leaves things a little hazy. God doesn't often give you the details and the foresight you'd like way ahead of time—who you're going to marry, where you're going to live, how many bambinos you'll bear, what exact job you'll have.

Here's why: God wants you to walk with Him *step by step*—and if He told all today, you wouldn't need Him tomorrow. True vision from God always comes mixed with a healthy dose of humility toward your ability to peer into the future. And of a minute-by-minute dependence on Him.

Now listen, you who say, "Today or tomorrow we will go to this or that city, spend a year there, carry on business and make money." Why, you do not even know what will happen tomorrow. What is your life? You are a mist that appears for a little while and then vanishes. Instead, you ought to say, "If it is the Lord's will, we will live and do this or that."

— J A M E S 4 : 1 3 – 1 5

WHAT'S YOUR PRIORITY?

PART EIGHT

PEERS AND POPULARITY

All your life you've been told what it takes to survive the high winds, frigid cold, and lack of oxygen as you scramble to the top of Mount Popularity. People promise that big biceps or the right bra size or bowing to the crowd's wishes will make you likeable.

Those things won't take you to the top.

And they won't keep you on top.

Think how quickly the fans who crowned Jesus "Mr. Jerusalem" changed their minds. Five days after the people praised Jesus, they became a pack of piranhas. They begged He be killed on a cross (Matthew 27:22–23).

Jesus knew that popularity scatters like snow flurries in a mountain wind. So He didn't play to the crowd. Instead, He made obeying God His ultimate aim (John 4:34).

The crowds that went ahead of him [Jesus] and those that followed shouted, "Hosanna to the Son of David!" "Blessed is he who comes in the name of the Lord!" "Hosanna in the highest!"

— MATTHEW 21:9

Lots of people think life is a popularity contest. The battle to be the best is so huge it seems normal. But in God's way of doing things, love is the law.

It's stupid not to realize some people are poised to bite you as they claw their way to the top. It's foolish not to know that some are so dangerous that you'd better scamper away when you see them coming (2 Timothy 3:2–5). But to love one another—that's the goal.

When people fight to be popular, both sides wind up bit. And they devour each other down to the last bite.

The whole law is made complete in this one command: "Love your neighbor as you love yourself." If you go on hurting each other and tearing each other apart, be careful, or you will completely destroy each other.

—GALATIANS 5:14–15 NCV

The ugliest people in the world are the ones who have perfected their outsides but neglected their insides. God—and people who are really worth impressing—know that your love for people and heart for God matter *more* than what you look like. God doesn't ask, "Did your hair turn out? Are your muscles gargantuan?" What He wants to know is: "Do you work hard? Can you be trusted? Do you have a good attitude? Are you kind?"

That doesn't mean you should trash your wardrobe and stop messing with your hair. God created you and wants you to take care of yourself. But He made you to please Him, not to be a slave to your looks.

*But the Lord said to Samuel, "Don't look at how
handsome Eliab is or how tall he is, because I have
not chosen him. God does not see the same way
people see. People look at the outside of a person, but
the Lord looks at the heart."*

— 1 SAMUEL 16:7 NCV

When you spend time with someone, you gradu-
ally resemble each other in how you dress and act.
The same thing happens spiritually. Who you hang
around with shapes what your character looks like.
When you spend time with Christ—talking with Him,
reading His Word, and being with His friends—you
begin to look like Him.

As you know Jesus better, people will see that you
look more and more like Him (1 Corinthians 3:18). No
one can fault you for being Jesus' look-alike ("against
such things there is no law"). If people criticize you
for being loving, joyful, peaceful, patient, kind, good,
faithful, gentle, and self-controlled, it's not your
problem.

*But when the Holy Spirit controls our lives, he will
produce this kind of fruit in us: love, joy, peace,
patience, kindness, goodness, faithfulness,
gentleness, and self-control.*

— GALATIANS 5:22–23 NLT

You don't have to be hyperspiritual to be what God wants you to be—and don't be duped by people who tell you differently.

Jesus doesn't instruct Christians to wear funny hats or to shave their heads. They don't necessarily hand out magazines at the mall or door-to-door. Their words don't always come out with "chapter 4, verse 12" attached. What makes a Christian different from other people is that he or she is (1) learning to love God totally ("love God with all your heart, soul and mind") and (2) learning to love others unselfishly ("love your neighbor as you love yourself").

True, your love for God may make others think you're weird. But your love for people may convince them that you're not. If your actions and words show that you care about others as much as you care about yourself, not everyone will call you *weird*. A lot of them may call you *friend*.

Jesus replied: "Love the Lord your God with all your heart and with all your soul and with all your mind." This is the first and greatest commandment. And the second is like it: "Love your neighbor as yourself."

—MATTHEW 22:37–39

A tug-of-war starts when a Christian is "yoked" to an unbeliever, lashed together like two horses joined to plow a field (2 Corinthians 6:14–15). A couple things can happen. The two of you can fight about how and where to plow and rip each other's heads off, or you can give in and let the non-Christian drag you down some row where you shouldn't go.

(By the way, forcing a non-Christian to go down your row isn't an option. Jesus doesn't *make* us come to him. He invites us. See Matthew 11:28–30.)

Going together, being best friends, dating, or marrying are all relationships that yoke. But other things can yoke you too. Sports teams, jobs, clubs, or activities that demand total commitment can also control you in a bad way.

No non-Christian will join with you completely in living your faith—in belonging to God and making Him and His people the most important things in your life. You won't head toward the same goals and standards.

Make no mistake: Jesus told Christians to reach out and enlarge God's family, and the only way that can happen is if you make friends with non-Christians, people who are outside the family. But God wants your closest friends to be ones you can pull together with to know and follow Him better.

So encourage each other and give each other strength, just as you are doing now.

— 1 THESSALONIANS 5:11 NCV

Since so many influences try to rip apart your

faith, you need to reinforce and rebuild yourself and your Christian friends through encouragement—talking, praying, sharing the excitement of being a Christian.

When getting together with other Christians conflicts with another activity, you might be able to reschedule one or the other. But when you can't, church shouldn't lose, even when that means disappointing advisors or friends, or missing future opportunities. Getting and giving encouragement is that important.

You'd be a fool to walk out on a football field to take on a whole team by yourself. You would look up, see eleven mammoths charging to stomp your body, and run crying off the field. Why do you think you can stay in the game alone as a Christian—where the opponent intends to kill you (1 Peter 5:8)? You need your team or you won't survive.

Think of ways to encourage one another to outbursts of love and good deeds. And let us not neglect our meeting together, as some people do, but encourage and warn each other. . . .

—HEBREWS 10:24–25 NLT

Life is like living underwater. Christian friends are your hose to the surface—not just for a whiff of fresh air, but for the lung-bulging oxygen you need to survive.

There's no such thing as a scuba tank that lets you

frolic through the deep waters of life all by your lonesome. You've got a lifeline, the air hose of friendship. That hose can kink, so you have to tend it carefully. But if you believe in Jesus, you're hooked up to His people. When you feel alone, ask God for Christian friends. And look around for His answer (1 Kings 19:1–18).

Flee the evil desires of youth, and pursue righteousness, faith, love and peace, along with those who call on the Lord out of a pure heart.

— 2 TIMOTHY 2:22

ETERNITY MEANS HEAVEN OR HELL

PART NINE

WHICH
DO YOU
CHOOSE?

God never meant for you to live clueless about the future—not just *your* future, but the *end-of-the-world* future.

Without understanding God's plans for wrapping up this world, you'll live in hopelessness. When you feel hurt by life, you'll blame God—not the rebellion that's the real cause of evil in this world. When you think life will never be fair or fun, you'll dread every tomorrow—and forget that God promises an eternity of more fun than you can fathom. When evil constantly succeeds all around you, you'll quit being good—and ignore the fact that God commands you to be faithful to the end. You'll rule your life by whims of what feels good rather than the long-term truth that good triumphs and evil is destroyed. And you'll live without a sense of God's ultimate protection through whatever you face, whenever you face it.

Yet the biggest reason God tells you about the end is so you'll ponder hard your relationship with Him. The most important fact you can know about what's ahead is whether *you* spend eternity with *Jesus*. You ought to know where you're gonna go.

Since everything around us is going to melt away,
what holy, godly lives you should be living! You
should look forward to that day and hurry it
along—the day when God will set the heavens on
fire and the elements will melt away in the flames.

—2 PETER 3:11–12 NLT

How can we be sure that Christ will come back? Or know exactly what His "second coming" will look like?

God's prophets accurately foresaw a slew of details about Christ's *first* coming. That gives us strong assurance we can trust biblical promises about the end of the world. We have wads of detail spoken by Jesus— Mr. Honesty—about His *return*.

The two basic points of what the Bible teaches about the end of the world are unmistakably clear. God wins. Satan loses. Read it again: Jesus triumphs—and the devil and his horde get served up on toast.

The outline of key end-time events also seems sure: Birthpains—Great Distress—Christ's Coming—Judgment—Eternity. Bible-obeying Christians do have different opinions about exactly how Christ's second coming plays out, but many would agree that these five elements reflect what God's Word predicts.

Plenty of preachers have wandered past the clear teachings of the Bible—picking antichrists and hyping dates for Christ's coming. That doesn't mean it's impossible to stay within the Bible's boundaries—that is, if we read to obey, read no more or less than what the Bible actually says, and read for the big points. Their *abuse* of Scripture doesn't rule out our responsible *use* of Scripture.

Get it straight up front: There will come a time that will be earth's ugliest hour. And there's a reason life gets so distressing. In the time of Great Distress (Tribulation) people not only follow false christs (Matthew 24:23–26), they chase *the* false christ. They fall for the ultimate alternative to God: the Antichrist.

Surprise: The term "Antichrist" appears nowhere in Revelation. But this shadowy figure pops up several times in Scripture.

- *He's the signal at the start of the Great Distress* (Matthew 24:15; Daniel 9:27; 11:31; 12:11).

- *He's the "man of lawlessness"* who arrives on the scene prior to Christ's second coming (2 Thessalonians 2:1, 3–4; 2:9–10).

- *He's the Antichrist in John's first and second letters*, the worst of a whole assortment of impostors (1 John 2:18, 22).

- *He's the beast of Revelation* (13:1, 3).

You might or might not live to see that. But the attitude of the Antichrist pops up all around you when any person, place, or thing tries to make itself more important than God.

But every spirit that does not acknowledge Jesus is not from God. This is the spirit of the antichrist, which you have heard is coming and even now is already in the world.

— 1 JOHN 4:3

You may have been told that the core of God's character is nasty, intolerant, and oozing angry judgment.

God's wrath lasts for a season—until evil is shattered. But the party He has planned for His people will last forever.

That party will be heavenly.

That party will be our home for eternity.

The back end of the Bible tells us more about heaven than any other place in the Bible. Revelation pictures heaven in a couple ways. *Heaven is like a city.* But this one doesn't have smog, grime, crime, or billions of cigarette butts lying around. It's a city made of gold, surrounded by a wall of God's protection. It's decorated with every kind of jewel. And it shines with God's glory, so no one needs a night-light—or the sun or moon, for that matter (Revelation 21:9–27). *Heaven is also like a garden.* A river of life gushes down the middle, flanked on both sides by the Tree of Life (Revelation 22:1–5).

As much as the world swirling around you might look different, Satan won't win. Evil will be conquered.

Little by little, Satan's rebellion against God is being beaten back. When the disciples went out and witnessed that in Jesus the kingdom of God had arrived, Satan fell like lightning from heaven (Luke 10:18). When Jesus died and rose He took away Satan's power to hold us hostage through sin and death. He "disarmed the powers and authorities" and "made a public spectacle of them, triumphing over them by the cross" (Colossians 2:15). And whenever one of us stops rebelling against God, Satan's army has one less soldier. Jesus has "rescued us from the dominion of darkness and brought us into the kingdom of the Son he loves, in whom we have redemption, the forgiveness of sins" (Colossians 1:13–14).

At the end of time Satan will at last be completely excluded from heaven. "He was hurled to the earth, and his angels with him" (Revelation 12:9). No one deserves to be hurled more than Satan. It's when he gets really hot—he knows his time is almost up (Revelation 12:12).

My dear children, you belong to God and have defeated them; because God's Spirit, who is in you, is greater than the devil, who is in the world.

— 1 JOHN 4:4 NCV

It's in Revelation 19 that Satan meets his match. Only, Satan's no match at all for Jesus, who rides in on a white stallion to bash Evil. His entrance is too suave not to read about firsthand:

> I saw heaven standing open and there before me was a white horse, whose rider is called Faithful and True. With justice he judges and makes war. His eyes are like blazing fire, and on his head are many crowns. He has a name written on him that no one knows but he himself. He is dressed in a robe dipped in blood, and his name is the Word of God. The armies of heaven were following him, riding on white horses and dressed in fine linen, white and clean. Out of his mouth comes a sharp sword with which to strike down the nations. "He will rule them with an iron scepter." He treads the winepress of the fury of the wrath of God Almighty. On his robe and on his thigh he has this name written: KING OF KINGS AND LORD OF LORDS. Revelation 19:11–16

It's more than a tad dramatic. Jesus rides into battle

flanked by the armies of heaven—apparently a host of angels. God's forces don't even need to join in. Jesus' weapon of choice is no thermonuclear warhead or neutron bomb. Not even His pinky. He strikes down the nations with His word, that sharp sword that comes out of His mouth.

Jesus merely speaks and His enemies go up in smoke.

At the name of Jesus every knee will bow, in heaven and on earth and under the earth, and every tongue will confess that Jesus Christ is Lord, to the glory of God the Father.
—PHILIPPIANS 2:10–11 NLT

Wrap together all that you've read about God's wrath against sin. You'd be warped not to get the message: God takes rebellion very seriously.

We all agree that Satan deserves every lick he gets— his thousand-year tumble into the bottomless pit, not to mention an eternity in a hot sulfur stew that reeks of rotten eggs. We even all agree that really bad people should get their due.

Here's the way harder part to hear: The whole human race is under God's judgment. We all answer to Him.

Strange. We think we can beat the system. Deke God. Outwit omniscience. But apart from Christ we all stand guilty. And trusting Christ is the only way to stand forgiven.

> *As the Scriptures say: "There is no one who always does what is right, not even one. There is no one who understands. There is no one who looks to God for help."*
>
> —ROMANS 3:10–11 NCV

Chew on these reality bites:

- *You can count on Christ's return.* " 'Behold, I am coming soon! My reward is with me, and I will give to everyone according to what he has done' " (Revelation 22:12).

- *You can't hide sin.* "O Lord, you have searched me and you know me. You know when I sit and when I rise; you perceive my thoughts from afar. You discern my going out and my lying down; you are familiar with all my ways" (Psalm 139:1–3).

- *You can't escape judgment.* "Man is destined to die once, and after that to face judgment" (Hebrews 9:27).

- *You can't talk your way out of punishment.* "Since you call on a Father who judges each man's work impartially, live your lives as strangers here in reverent fear" (1 Peter 1:17). That's addressed to Christians.

- *You won't enjoy the punishment.* "If anyone's name was not found written in the book of life, he was thrown into the lake of fire" (Revelation 20:15).

*Don't be misled. Remember that you can't ignore
God and get away with it. You will always
reap what you sow!*

—GALATIANS 6:7 NLT

The good things we've had here on Planet Earth
will be like baby mush compared to the unending
feast of heaven. What we've enjoyed of God's creation—music, nature, color, beauty—will be given to us
in abundance, with mind-boggling intensity. We can
expect incredible surprises, because our dreams now
are warped by sin. But be sure of this: Whatever we
find in heaven will totally satisfy, as if God were to say,
"You think that's good? Try this!"

Even better than the place will be the people. God's
friends will live in His peace—no enemies, no popularity contests, no prejudice or jealousy, no ugly
names or biting words.

But the real life of this eternal party will be God himself. He'll live with us the way He's wanted to since He
created this world—with no doubt, fear, or sin sepa-
rating us from Him. We'll begin to know God as well
as He knows us, and celebrate Him for giving us an
eternity of friendship with himself and His people.

God wants *you* in heaven. And if God is your friend,
there's no better place to be.

*I heard a loud shout from the throne, saying,
"Look, the home of God is now among his people!
He will live with them, and they will be his people.
God himself will be with them. He will remove all
of their sorrows, and there will be no more death or
sorrow or crying or pain. For the old world
and its evils are gone forever."*
— REVELATION 21:3–4 NLT

EVANGELISM IS GIVING IT AWAY

PART TEN

HOW ELSE THEY GONNA KNOW?

Unless you went through school with your head in a bucket, you've watched peers toss away school, ditch their families, and torch their brains with drugs. Why do they choose to destroy themselves and others? Lots of times it's because they've been pushed to the fringes of life. Ignored. Trivialized. Neglected. Abused.

It might have been tough to treat people well in high school, to act any differently than the crowd all around you. But you're a big boy or girl now. And it's time to start fresh and think hard about how you're going to treat people for the rest of your life.

People need to know that God invites them to significance. They can know Him. They can do things that matter—feed a hungry person, comfort an abused child, show classmates and teachers and bosses what a real Christian looks like, help introduce people to God—and change people's lives *forever*. Life lived close to Christ is a life-altering substance, a world-changing power. God fiercely believes in them. And in you.

Working on your own you can't make a dent in the world. God working through you can change the world around you. God working through you and other believers can change the planet.

Your love for one another will prove to the world that you are my disciples.

—JOHN 13:35 NLT

If you follow Jesus, sooner or later people figure it out.

And sooner or later someone doesn't like it. They laugh at you or slam you or just ignore you.

You don't have to hang yourself out for them to hate you. The Bible doesn't say, "Go ye forth and rubbeth thy faith in thy neighbor's face and shoveth it down thy acquaintence's throat." But it does coach you to be honest and unashamed: "Live such good lives among the pagans that, though they accuse you of doing wrong, they may see your good deeds and glorify God" (1 Peter 2:12).

Those are words from the guy who three times said he didn't know Jesus—only hours after he swore he would go with Jesus to prison and death (Luke 22:31–34).

Soldiers had swept in and captured Jesus, who would soon die. Like a cornered dog, Peter lashed out. He flashed a sword and whacked off a servant's ear (John 18:10). He feared for his own life and tried to hide. Then, just as Jesus had predicted, Peter claimed three times not to know Him.

Notice the change in Peter's life? It can be the same in yours.

Then Peter remembered that the Lord had said,
"Before the rooster crows tomorrow morning, you
will deny me three times." And Peter left the
courtyard, crying bitterly.
—LUKE 22:61–62 NLT

You can't tell people about Jesus solely by doing spiritual charades, motioning and miming to make your point. Having the truth inside your head doesn't do anyone any good if you don't show it and—at the right time—*speak* it. In the Bible, truth isn't something just to *believe*. It's something you *speak*, *live*, and *do*. Christians speak up for truth because they love truth, do truth, and live truth.

It's a simple formula: *Speak the truth*, but do it *in love*.

If you ever find yourself speaking about Christ in make-people-spew *pushiness* or in make-people-want-to-clobber-you *anger*, you're almost surely in the wrong spot at the wrong time. When you love the people you're talking to, you bend over backward to make things clear to them—and at the same time you don't get bent out of shape when they say something unkind to or about you. They might insult you. Contradict you. Imply you're brainless or evil. If you're speaking the truth in love you'll ignore those zingers and focus on your goal of talking about Christ.

Big Hint: Radical commitment to Jesus doesn't make you beat people over the head with a thousand-pound Bible. In fact, if your zeal isn't directed by wisdom and study, it becomes a *detriment to the gospel*. Here's your check: Does your method of sharing Christ move people closer to God? If you mostly make people mad and turn them off to God, you need to rethink your strategy.

*Speaking the truth with love, we will grow up in
every way into Christ, who is the head.*

—EPHESIANS 4:15 NCV

Paul said that "faith comes from hearing the message, and the message is heard through the word of Christ" (Romans 10:17). There's no way around it: People can't hear about Christ and chase after Him if you don't split your lips and speak up. But what should you say?

That's a problem.

Suppose you're a guy in love with the most beauteous girl ever. You're totally gone. It's a godly relationship with an authentic woman of God. So how would you explain that to others? You could say what she's like—rattle off her shoe size, her mother's maiden name, and what kind of cat her dog likes to eat. You could say how she makes your heart rumble. Or you could explain how you found her. You've got loads to say!

It's the same with God. There's so much to tell. Every bit of it sheds light on God. Your friends—whether they're friends here, there, or anywhere—need to know *who God is*. It's persuasive if they grasp *what He's done for you*. But somewhere along the way they need to get their facts straight. They need to know *how they can have a relationship with God*.

This is good and pleases God our Savior, for he
wants everyone to be saved and to understand the
truth. For there is only one God and one Mediator
who can reconcile God and people. He is the man
Christ Jesus.

— 1 TIMOTHY 2:3–5 NLT

You can tell people here, there, and everywhere about Jesus. You can explain what the Bible says about what it means to be a Christian. You can show God's love by being a servant. But it's not enough for people to hear about Christ—even to see Him living in you. They need to understand and act on what they hear—to receive and follow. That won't happen without God's working inside them. " 'No one can come to me,' " Jesus said, " 'unless the Father who sent me draws him' " (John 6:44).

You'll go nuts if you think you can make people follow Christ. You'll get pushy and ugly and try to hijack God's job. It's the Holy Spirit who does the real work inside the people you talk to. He "testifies" to Christ, making real everything you explain. He convinces people of the wrongness of their sin, of God's powerful goodness, and Christ's defeat of Satan (John 16:7–11).

But I will send you the Counselor—the Spirit of
truth. He will come to you from the Father and will
tell you all about me.

—JOHN 15:26 NLT

There's a Far Side cartoon that shows a bunch of beanbags in a living room. Typical of *Far Side* cartoons, the beanbags are alive. Out the beanbag family's front window you see two people carrying book bags walk toward the front door. Papa beanbag says to his family, "Look out! The Jehovah's Witnesses are coming! Make like beanbags!"

That's how most folks—including Christians—handle the dudes at their door. Dim the lights. Mute the TV. Make like nobody is home.

Maybe, in a way, nobody *is* home.

In the meantime, these folks—people trapped in false religions, hanging on to false hope that they belong to God, figuring they'll spend eternity with Him in heaven—walk by our homes, carrying Bibles and wanting to talk God.

Maybe you witness in class or at work. Maybe you tell people around town about Jesus. Maybe you've even done short-term missions trips. *Don't stop doing those things.* But trudging through your neighborhood, donking your doorbell, these people come right to you. You've got a mission field on your doorstep.

Turn on the lights.

Talk to them.

Here I am! I stand at the door and knock. If anyone hears my voice and opens the door, I will come in and eat with him, and he with me.

—REVELATION 3:20

People think Christians are hypocrites. And people think Christians are nuns hiding from the world. Hardly. You can show them differently.

To people who think you're a hypocrite, you can showcase love. Your generation can show the world's broken pagans what it looks like to have an intact family—loving your parents, spouse, and kids. You can demonstrate God's love for your community, country, and the whole of human civilization.

To people who think you're a coward, you can go over the walls of your church and show them that Jesus is more than superintendent of Sunday school. Let them know that God is Lord over all. He has answers to the absolutely huge intellectual and social issues coming to challenge the faith of your generation of Christians: euthanasia, cloning, race relations, biochemistry and personality, postmodern thought, artificial intelligence, the age of the universe, the downfall of evolution, and the rise of intelligent design.

People who do not believe are living all around you and might say that you are doing wrong. Live such good lives that they will see the good things you do and will give glory to God on the day when Christ comes again.

—1 PETER 2:12 NCV

Give answers. There's so much to know about God that you'll be learning for the rest of your life— eternal life, that is. But the *basics* are your starting point when you talk about God with people who don't know God. There's no magic formula. Still, these are the points to get across:

- *God*—There's only one.

- *Jesus*—He's fully God.

- *Holy Spirit*—Believers are empowered by a Holy *He*, not a force or a feeling or a Holy *it*.

- *Grace*—Salvation is God's total gift to us.

- *Faith*—It's our right response to God's promises, especially the promise of eternal life.

- *Good works*—We live holy lives to say thanks to God, not to win His approval.

- *Bible*—The Bible sums up our faith and doesn't need supplements.

When you talk to someone who doesn't know God, your goal isn't to bash what they believe. Or show how street-wise you are about non-Christian beliefs. It's to pass on the hope we have in Christ.

When you put Christ first in your life, it's going to show. Sure, you might not be the boldest, outgoing-est witness ever to walk the earth, but when you love Jesus it *always* shows in some way. Sooner or later you find yourself answering questions from people around you like, "Hey, why aren't you scared of the future?" Or "Why aren't you a basket case when things get bad?" No matter where you go, you can *always* be ready to explain why you trust God.

*But respect Christ as the holy Lord in your hearts.
Always be ready to answer everyone who asks you
to explain about the hope you have, but answer in a
gentle way and with respect. Keep a clear conscience
so that those who speak evil of your good life in
Christ will be made ashamed.*

— 1 PETER 3:15–16 NCV

More Resources for Tackling Your Future

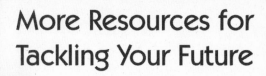

UNDERSTANDING GOD'S WILL FOR YOUR LIFE

Happiness, a good career, good friends, and closeness with God are desires of everyone's heart. This book explains that God also desires to give these things to you—He even promises a specific plan for you to experience each of them. There's no catch, but there is a condition, a condition you can't afford to miss!

God's Will, God's Best
by Josh McDowell and Kevin Johnson

HOW YOUR TALENTS, GIFTS, AND PERSONALITY ADD UP TO YOU!

Written just for teens seeking answers to their future, this important book (part of the LifeKeys resources for spiritual discovery) explains how to use who you are to do what God designed you to do. Unique inventories help you understand your values, passions, talents, and gifts better to get a clearer idea of what to do with your life.

Find Your Fit
by Jane Kise and Kevin Johnson

⬧BETHANYHOUSE

11400 Hampshire Ave.S., Bloomington MN 55438
www.bethanyhouse.com   1-800-328-6109